FACEBOOK LIVE EMPIRE

By Joseph Goldberg

Copyright © 2021 by Joseph Goldberg
All rights reserved, including the right to reproduce this book or portions thereof in any form whatsoever

LEGAL DISCLAIMER:

The Publisher has strived to be as accurate and complete as possible in the creation of this report, even though he does not warrant or represent at any time that the contents within are accurate due to the rapidly changing nature of the Internet.

Any viewed slights of specific persons, individuals, or companies are unintended. The purpose of this book is to educate, and there are no guarantees of income, sales or results implied. The publisher/author/reseller can, for that reason, not be held accountable for any bad results you may attain when implementing the methods or when following any standards set out for you in this book.

The author and publisher shall have neither liability nor responsibility to any person or entity concerning any loss or damage caused or alleged to be caused directly or indirectly by this book

INTRODUCTION	6
CHAPTER 1	7
FACEBOOK LIVE 101	7
What is Facebook Live?	7
Is Facebook Live worth it?	8
Facebook Live on any Device	8
CHAPTER 2	10
THE BENEFITS OF USING FACEBOOK LIVE FOR YOUR BUSINESS	10
Main Benefits of Facebook Live	10
Questions and Answers.	11
Great throughout a Pandemic.	12
Share Product or Service updates.	12
Behind the Scenes.	12
Facebook Live is well developed.	13
Your Event Saved.	13
Top-Notch Analytics.	14
You get Eight Hours.	14
Interaction.	15
CHAPTER 3	16
GETTING STARTED WITH FACEBOOK LIVE	16
You require the ideal Equipment	16
Check your Internet Connection	17
Consider Third-Party Tools	17
Create a Plan for your Event	18
Get Ready for your Live Event	19
Time for your Broadcast	20
When you go Life	20
Scheduling a Facebook Live event.	21
CHAPTER 4	23
TIPS FOR A GREAT FACEBOOK LIVE EVENT	23
Natural Lighting	23
Produce as many Practice Recordings as you require	24
Record Horizontally with Mobile	24
Be Human	25
Smiling is a Must	25
Request Interaction	25
Put your Mistakes to great use	26
Get aid with Questions	26
Have a Call to Action at the end	27

Add a Custom Thumbnail — 27
Add Captions to your Event Video — 28
Pin your Video Post — 28
Consider Boosting your Event Video — 28
Usage Facebook Analytics — 29

CHAPTER 5 — 30

FACEBOOK LIVE NEW FEATURES FOR 2021 — 30
The Trimming Feature — 30
Duration now Extended — 30
Watch Parties — 31

CHAPTER 6 — 32

GREAT CONTENT IDEAS FOR YOUR FACEBOOK LIVE EVENTS — 32
The How-To Event — 32
New Product Launches — 32
Professional Interviews — 32
Services Or Product Demonstrations — 33
Ask Me Anything or Q&A — 34

CHAPTER 7 — 35

CREATING THE MOST ENGAGING FACEBOOK LIVE EVENTS — 35
Develop your Event around what your Audience desires — 35
Arrange your Event and Promote it first — 36
Prepare your Environment — 36
Timing is everything — 37
Keep Updating your Audience — 38
Interaction is King — 38
Utilize your Events to Build Relationships — 39
Promote your Video after the event — 39
What can you do better? — 40

CHAPTER 8 — 41

HOW TO USE FACEBOOK LIVE TO DRIVE LEADS AND SALES — 41
Usage Promotions and Discounts during your Events — 41
Use Prompts for Lead Generation — 41
Show your Products or Services — 42
Strong Call to Action — 43
Ask your Viewers to Share your Event — 43

CHAPTER 9 — 45

FACEBOOK LIVE BEST PRACTICES — 45
Understand what Facebook Live is — 45
Advantages of Facebook Live — 45
Get going the right way with Facebook Live — 45

Usage Proven methods to develop a Great Facebook Live Event	46
Maintain to date with New Features	46
Usage Good Content Ideas	46
Produce Engaging Facebook Live Events	46
Drive Leads and Sales with Facebook Live	47

CONCLUSION   **48**

INTRODUCTION

Facebook is the most significant social network and you can discover great deals of potential consumers for your business with it. Using Facebook Live events is a great way to connect with your audience. The majority of businesses do not use Facebook Live because they don't value the advantages of it or they think that it is too made complex.

By using the strategies in this guide you can get ahead of your rivals and use Facebook Live to your advantage. You will learn what you need to do and what you require to avoid here so make certain to read it all and execute what you find out.

We have worked hard to offer you everything that you need to know to use the Facebook Live platform to increase your brand and drive more leads and sales. You will discover proven methods to get the best outcomes with Facebook Live. Engagement with your audience is necessary and this guide will reveal to you how to attain that.

Other businesses have attempted utilizing Facebook Live and failed. We do not desire you to make the same mistakes that they did so follow the steps in this guide and you will maximize your chances of success.

CHAPTER 1

FACEBOOK LIVE 101

Facebook is the largest social network website worldwide. At the time of composing, Facebook has 2.7 billion users, and every month, it receives around 25 billion visitors. The majority of these visitors have Facebook accounts. The factor for sharing this with you is because a percentage of those Facebook users would be perfect consumers for your business.

It is simpler to find potential consumers on Facebook than with other platforms. You can target people by their age variety, their income, their place, their gender, their interests, and more. So in this guide, we will show you how you can leverage the power of Facebook and in particular, Facebook Live to promote your brand.

What is Facebook Live?

In April 2016, Facebook released its streaming video service called Facebook Live. With this service, you can hold a live occasion with your target market through your business page on Facebook.

Although Facebook Live has been around for over 4 years, a couple of businesses benefit from it to increase the awareness of their brand name. There could be several various reasons for this however the bottom line is that they are losing out on a fantastic opportunity.

Facebook users like live events. All Facebook Live occasions are taped and after the occasion, these become available on your Facebook page. So if any of your fans missed the live occasion they will have the ability to see the replay.

When a Facebook Live occasion has started, alerts of the occasion can appear in the news feed of your followers. This can also happen as soon as the vent has finished. This is a great feature as some individuals will forget that they planned to go to the live event. It is likewise handy to those fans that we're unable to participate for some reason.

Facebook has made a variety of modifications to its algorithm to give Facebook Live occasions a higher concern. So now there is an even higher chance of Facebook users seeing your live video streaming occasion.

Is Facebook Live worth it?

Yes, it certainly is! Video marketing is a lot more reliable than text-based material. Individuals like to see videos online. Just YouTube has more video views than Facebook does. Video is an excellent way to develop and promote your brand name.

However, it gets even better. Adweek has information to prove that a Facebook Live occasion gets three times greater engagement levels than an occasion video that has been completed (a recording or replay). Adweek likewise mentions that the engagement levels for Facebook Live videos are five times higher than they are for an image post.

So if you are looking to offer your brand a boost, get more leads for your business and make more sales then Facebook Live is a great method to do it. If you have hesitated to make videos before and show your face on a video camera then you need to overcome this. With Facebook Live you can put your brand on the map.

Facebook Live on any Device

It doesn't matter if you use a desktop-like a laptop computer or a mobile device such as a mobile phone or tablet, you can produce a Facebook Live event. There is a basic process to go through depending on what device you want to use.

With a laptop or home computer simply use your Internet internet browser (Chrome, Firefox, Opera, etc) and login to Facebook as you would generally. At the top of your news feed, you will see a box with "What's on your mind" so click this. Then choose the "Live Video" alternative.

There are Facebook apps readily available for both Android and iOS-powered mobile devices. You can quickly find these at the Google Play Store or the Apple Store. Download the app on your device and install it.

With an Android device, you will require to tap on "What's on your mind" and then tap on "Go Live". With an iOS device, it is somewhat various. Discover "What's on your mind" at the top of your feed and then tap the icon for video recording that will likewise say "Live Video".

Whatever device you utilize you just follow these steps now. You will require to offer your live occasion a name and supply a description about it (this is optional however suggested). You can also submit a video thumbnail.

The next step is to choose the audience for your Facebook Live occasion. Click or tap on "Next" and when you are ready to go simply click or tap on "Go Live". You require to be aware that there is a 4-hour time frame for Facebook Live videos.

This is more than enough time for your occasion. Nobody is going to want to sit through a 4 hour Facebook Live session no matter how good it is. We will discuss this in more detail in a later chapter. In the next chapter, we will talk about the advantages of using Facebook Live for your business ...

CHAPTER 2

THE BENEFITS OF USING FACEBOOK LIVE FOR YOUR BUSINESS

Businesses all over the world are experiencing great results with video marketing. Surveys recommend that businesses that utilize videos to promote their brand name and their product or services experience nearly 50% higher earnings than those that do not utilize video.

One survey exposed that nearly 60% of their individuals specified that video marketing supplied them with the best return of all material marketing types. In the very same study, 78% of the individuals stated that they chose live video as it allowed a deeper connection with their audience.

Main Benefits of Facebook Live

Here are the primary advantages for businesses to utilize Facebook Live as we see it. There are others too and we will discuss the advantages in more information:

- You can reach the largest audience worldwide utilizing a website that they utilize all of the time-- Facebook
- Facebook Live has some outstanding audience engagement functions consisting of 2 unique ones which are live reactions and commenting real-time
- Businesses can use Facebook Live for internal meetings or external conferences with clients etc
- Video performance analytics provide exceptional insight.
- You can use paid Facebook ads to increase your live events to reach more prospective audiences.

When you use Facebook Live to get in touch with your audience you bring a real human touch. You are not a faceless company that customers and prospective consumers do not know the people behind it. This is very essential for establishing trust and developing credibility for your brand name.

A Facebook Live event supplies a "face to face" chance that text posts and image posts can not accomplish. You can have a single host or introduce other members of your business to your audience.

Questions and Answers.

Another benefit of holding a Facebook Live event is that you can hold a real-time question and answer session. This will improve your engagement and it is a good concept to let people understand that there will be a Q & A session before the event going live.

People like to ask questions. It is most likely that a lot of individuals going to will have their questions addressed by other attendees asking the questions. This is great as not everybody feels comfy about asking questions on a live video stream.

You can either take questions as they turn up or request that people wait up until completion of the event and you will respond to all questions then. By waiting till the end, you will increase the possibilities of your followers viewing the whole event.

Some businesses established recurring Facebook Live events where they take questions as they emerge. Recurring events are great if you have a lot of content to share with your audience. Is finest of the material is various each time and not a repeat of what you have presented currently.

Great throughout a Pandemic.

At the time of writing this guide, the world remains in the grip of the Covid-19 pandemic. Some nations and states are in overall lockdown so they can not go to physical events. So the interest in your Facebook Live event is most likely to be greater in this scenario.

Applications like Zoom have seen a significant boost in users over the past few months. So participating in a live event on Facebook will not be an issue for many people. After the pandemic, we estimate that the need for online events will remain strong so the time to begin is right now.

Share Product or Service updates.

A Facebook Live event is an excellent way for you to share the current info about your product or services. Do you have a brand-new service or product? Have you made enhancements to existing products or services? Are there any unique discount rates that you are using today?

In some markets, things change rapidly. If this applies to your business then you can let your followers learn about the changes with a Facebook Live event. Your audience will value you keeping them informed and will spread the word for you.

Behind the Scenes.

People wish to know who lags your business. They wish to see faces and know the names of your group. If it is possible (pandemic allowing) you can shoot a live event during your opening hours and offer your fans a tour of your business.

Interviews with other staff members are a great strategy as well. Your audience can see that your group is completely dedicated to supplying them with the highest quality of service. All of this will help to develop you as a brand that cares about its customers.

Facebook Live is well developed.

Nowadays a lot of social platforms use live event streaming. The advantage of Facebook Live is that it has been around for a couple of years now and has gone through a variety of enhancements to make it much better and repair any concerns.

Facebook Live has some fantastic functions that other live platforms do not have such as their innovative alert system which will let your audience understand when an event is going live. You likewise can promote your Facebook Live event ahead of time now.

At the end of the day, people like Facebook and trust it. The numbers do not lie here-- no other social network comes close to user numbers and traffic. So holding your live event on Facebook is the smart thing to do.

Your Event Saved.

Facebook will tape your live event and turn it into a typical video post on your Facebook page. This suggests that you can continue to use it for promo after your event is over. There are always going to be some people that can not attend a live event so you can use the replay to them so that they don't miss out.

If you are running a series of live events on Facebook then anyone that was not in from the start can go through the recordings on your Facebook page to catch up. You can likewise increase your tape-recorded video posts to acquire more followers and possible viewers of your next live event.

Top-Notch Analytics.

For any online marketing that you do, you must have the analytics offered to see how well things went. When you utilize Facebook Live for your events you will have access to very well-established analytics. Not just will you be able to see the thorough video analytics that Facebook offers but likewise there is live analytics that you can access.

The info that you can anticipate seeing with live analytics consists of:

- Several live audiences (peak).
- Reactions to your event.
- Shares of your event.
- Comments.
- Your total reach.

You need to understand which content works best for your business and the analytics in Facebook will help you to discover this. When you have a couple of Facebook Live events under your belt you will be able to see which events your audience reacted the very best to and make more of these types of discussions.

You get Eight Hours.

Other social platforms offer live event streaming such as Twitter, Instagram, and Periscope. These are fine if you want to provide brief live videos. With Facebook Live you have a limitation of 8 hours which is more than enough time for a business to get its message through to followers.

The other thing to keep in mind here is that Facebook users are used to investing quite a bit of time on the platform. So they are most likely to spend time for a live event than they could be with other platforms. The interface with Facebook is likewise ideally developed for a live event.

Interaction.

With a Facebook Live event, there is a great deal of opportunity for interaction. Unlike other social platforms that use live events, you can write a caption for your live video as a way to attract more audiences to it.

When you host a Facebook Live event the interface will show real-time comments. You can respond to these comments as they arrive. Conversing in the minute like this will drive engagement levels higher and assist you to develop a strong relationship with your audience. In the next chapter, we will discuss how, to begin with, Facebook Live ...

CHAPTER 3

GETTING STARTED WITH FACEBOOK LIVE

Some people are apprehensive about hosting a Facebook Live event and there is no requirement for this. It is really simple to get started if you follow the guidance in this chapter. We will discuss exactly what you need to do. You should have a Facebook page currently set up for your business.

Trying to run an efficient Facebook Live event with a personal Facebook account is not recommended. There are numerous benefits to having a free Facebook page so if you don't have one yet then produce this very first.

You require the ideal Equipment

While it is possible to utilize your mobile phone or tablet to host your Facebook Live event there are better methods to do it. Modern mobile devices do have high-quality video recorders but the microphones frequently leave a lot to be wanted. Likewise holding a mobile device in your hand when you are tape-recording is undesirable as you are going to produce a shaky video.

You are running a business and wish to improve your brand, generate leads and sales. So wouldn't you want to develop the highest quality Facebook Live videos that you can? No one will expect you to develop a Hollywood design event but they will appreciate high-quality video (without any shaking) and audio.

If your video is of poor quality then people will leave the event rapidly. The same opts for poor-quality audio. Some guides suggest that you can use the built-in webcam and microphone in your laptop but these tend to be of inferior quality.

Be prepared to invest a little in great recording equipment. You can get an HD quality web webcam for around $50 nowadays and a good quality USB microphone for around $100.

Then there is the lighting in your home or business properties. Poor lighting will diminish the quality of your Facebook Live event so purchase good lighting for less than $100.

Check your Internet Connection

You want the very best Internet connection possible for a Facebook Live event. If you use WiFi to connect to the Internet as lots of businesses do then check your connection before starting with your live event.

If other individuals share your Internet connection then it is a good concept to ask to avoid downloads or any other bandwidth intense activities while you are using Facebook Live. You can utilize a booster for your WiFi network to boost the signal to where you are located if this is needed.

The last thing that you wish to occur during your event is to lose your Internet connection. If your WiFi signal is weak then this can cause your video to cut in or out so ensure that you have the strongest possible signal. It might be worth your while to use a direct cable television connection to your router to remove the use of WiFi.

Consider Third-Party Tools

Although you can develop your Facebook Live events without the requirement for any other tools, a lot of businesses are finding that some 3rd party services help them to produce a better live event. They can offer extra functions such as:

- More than one presenter

- Sharing of your screen
- Including custom graphics and titles

For instance, you can use Zoom to stream your presentation to Facebook which is great because Zoom uses better administrative tools for inviting people to sign up for the event. Your event still happens under Facebook Live. It also has some great functions that are not readily available with native Facebook Live streams.

Create a Plan for your Event

We do not advise that you wing it with Facebook Live. This is OKAY if you wish to captivate your loved ones on your personal Facebook account but it is far from ideal for a business presentation.

You require to consider what you wish to attain with your live event. Will it is a one-off event or will you develop a series of events? Bear in mind that you do not have to go live straight away with your event. You can utilize the scheduling function to set up your Facebook Live event to 7 days ahead of time.

By arranging your event for later you will have the time to develop a test event using the Facebook Live Producer function. If you have never hosted a live event online before then we strongly advise that you take advantage of this function.

Give believed to the circulation of your event discussion. Strategy what you are going to state and do throughout the event. If you prepare to invite visitors to your event then write an introduction script for this.

You don't need to produce a complete script for your event if you do not wish to. What we do recommend is that you produce a list of things that you wish to talk about offering. Checking out from a script can look and sound unnatural so just be guided by your discussion points list if you can.

Another crucial decision is whether you will answer questions as they show up or you tell your audience that you will answer them at the end of the centerpiece. Question and answer sessions are typically very popular so having a session at the end should increase your chances of people remaining for the centerpiece.

Get Ready for your Live Event

Make certain that you are gotten ready for your live event. There are several things that you can get ready for depending upon the nature of your event. Lighting and background noise are always crucial elements.

If you are hosting the event in your home or workplace then you will have control over your environment and you can guarantee excellent lighting and very little background noise. With an event outdoors this is not so simple naturally. Natural light is usually adequate for an excellent stream however it can be hard to remove background noise. Pick your place thoroughly.

Utilize a device like a tripod to hold your electronic camera or mobile device constant when you are tape-recording. A shaky video is not something that your followers want to see. Holding a microphone is OKAY if you are outdoors. For indoor shoots utilize a microphone stand.

You wish to keep diversions down to a minimum when you are recording your Facebook Live events. Let others understand that they must not interrupt you unless there is an emergency. Put your phone on quiet as constant notification sounds can irritate viewers.

There is nothing incorrect with tape-recording your Facebook Live event in the house however you need to be conscious that distractions are more likely there if you have kids and animals for example. Although it can be amusing for kids or animals to appear suddenly in your live sessions it is not the expert image that you want for your business.

Time for your Broadcast

At this moment you are ready for your live event. If you are utilizing a 3rd party service such as Zoom you will need to follow the particular instructions from them to begin your live event. For native Facebook Live events follow these actions:

If you are using a desktop or laptop then login to your Facebook account and navigate to the Facebook page you have set up for your business. Scroll down to the "Create Post" box and straight below this there is another box with the very first icon on the left called "Live". Click on this and then decide if you are going to tape now or schedule.

You will then need to "Share to a Page You Manage" from the dropdown menu. Use the 2nd dropdown menu to pick your Facebook page. Now you can include a title for your live event and a description. This is very essential so use an attractive copy here. After this, you can tag people, add a feeling, add a donation button and check in to a location.

If you want to make a test broadcast (always an excellent concept) then you will see a choice for this at the bottom. By using this function you can check your presentation and interactive components before you go live.

With a mobile device, the actions are similar. On the author page, simply tap on "Live" to start the procedure. You can then include your title and description and do things like tag buddies, include contribution buttons and include a sensation.

When you go Life

When you first begin your Facebook Live event you need to give your audience a small amount of time to join the event before you begin. Do not make this too long or those that have currently joined will become agitated.

As people join your event make sure to invite them and say "hi". Start the interaction here by asking people for their places. You can likewise ask them what they want to attain by attending your event

Try to find the best comments from those that have joined your event and pin them so that they appear at the top of the comments box. Tell your audience that you will either take and address questions as you go along or have a specific Q & A session at the end of the primary presentation.

When it is time for you to end your event be sure to thank people for attending and tell them that the event is ending. At the proper time, struck the "Finish" button and your event will end.

Scheduling a Facebook Live event.

You can always arrange your Facebook Live event for up to 7 days beforehand. Navigate to "Publishing Tools" and then select "Video Library" and after this hit "Live". This will bring up a screen that contains your broadcasting credentials.

If you are using a 3rd party service such as Zoom then you will require to utilize the information on this page so that you establish an appropriate connection. You can write a persuasive title and description to entice people to attend your event now.

Now go to the Facebook Live "Scheduling Tool" and hit "Schedule" which ought to be at the bottom right. You will see a sneak peek of your event here and you can include an image (this is a great concept) along with set up the date and time of your event.

Apart from giving you more time to promote your Facebook Live event, the schedule will create a "lobby" where people that join your event 3 minutes before it begins can engage with each other.

You can get a link to your Facebook Live event and use this to release details about it on your website or blog site. If you have an email list then you can send out e-mails with the link consisted of to drive more audiences. People can request a pointer and then get a notice a couple of minutes before your event is arranged to go live.

In the next chapter, we will go over some fantastic ideas to help you to develop an excellent Facebook Live event ...

CHAPTER 4

TIPS FOR A GREAT FACEBOOK LIVE EVENT

Once you have devoted yourself to using Facebook Live as an excellent marketing tool for your business and brand name you must use it in the most efficient method to optimize your possibilities of producing leads and making sales.

People that view your Facebook Live events are going to evaluate you on how well you come across and the quality of the video. So we have some suggestions for you to follow here to offer the very best Facebook Live event that you can. These suggestions are easy to follow and implement so please use them all.

Natural Lighting

If your face is not clear on your Facebook Live video then you will drive people away. There have been a lot of Facebook Live videos released where the lighting was incorrect and the host was out of focus or the light was just too bright.

Among the biggest errors that people make with their Facebook Live recordings is that they place themselves with their back to a window. When you do this the sunlight being available from the window will dominate the video image which you want to avoid at all costs.

So the very first idea here is to deal with the window if you are tape-recording throughout the daytime as the natural light will truly improve the video image. You as the host will be clear on the video which is what you desire. If you are a glasses wearer then think about taking these off as they can trigger a distracting glare.

Produce as many Practice Recordings as you require

This is particularly important if you have never hosted a live streaming event before. When you create practice videos you can go over them afterward and see what you are doing right and what you are doing wrong.

You can examine the quality of the video for lighting. If there are shadows or too much brightness or darkness you can alter your environment to enhance these elements. Likewise, check that the audio is crisp and clear. Are you too loud or too peaceful?

It can be quite overwhelming to watch yourself presenting for the very first time but after a while, you will overcome this. Inspect to see if your video flows nicely which you come across as friendly. With practice videos, you can straighten out the bumps before you go live.

Record Horizontally with Mobile

If you are going to utilize a mobile phone to tape-record your Facebook Live event then we strongly advise that you tape horizontally. Those vertically recorded videos just do not look good and you require to remember that your viewers will need to put up with this for however long your event lasts.

Horizontally recorded videos look much better in a Facebook feed. The other thing that you can do with your mobile phone is to include a nice filter and utilize other tools to boost the video quality. If you have the option of using a desktop or laptop computer with a high-quality web camera and microphone instead of a mobile device we will always recommend that you do this.

Be Human

Do not miss out on the opportunity to form a great human connection with your Facebook Live events. Inform your audience of some interesting aspects of your life and attempt to keep the event on an individual level as much as you can.

Ensure that any personal information you reveal is positive. No one is going to wish to listen to you complaining about how bad your life is (unless you are doing this for comedic effect). Your audience has sufficient issues of their own to handle not to mention listening to yours.

Smiling is a Must

If you have an unpleasant or too major face on when you make your Facebook Live recordings then you will drive people away quicker than you can believe. You need to smile as much as possible when you are on cam as this will make your audience feel happy about watching you.

Discover to talk to a smile too. If your speech is unfriendly or monotone then people will become bored extremely quickly and most likely leave. You want to stimulate your audiences with your character and inspire them. If it matters, tell your audience how you overcame particular challenges and give them the self-confidence that they can do it too.

Request Interaction

Always remember that Facebook loves posts that have a lot of views, comments, likes, and shares and will prioritize these in news feeds. Facebook has fine-tuned their algorithm to recognize popular content and assist you to make it a lot more popular for free.

So ask your viewers to interact with you. Ask your audiences to ask questions in the comments area and likewise ask to like and share your event. You can drive more interaction by having a competitor or a gift where your audience needs to make comments to win.

As you are making your discussion, ask your audience questions. This helps you to check that they are understanding your message and also provides your interactivity a good increase. Make it as simple as possible for viewers to react. Don't ask questions that require a long answer.

Put your Mistakes to great use

You are going to make mistakes recording a live event. As you become more knowledgeable you will probably make fewer errors but they are going to take place. If you get a bit tongue connected then don't be up to pieces! Make fun of this with your audience and proceed.

People watching a live event are not anticipating excellence. Some of them look forward to the errors because they provide an enjoyable break. So you require to find out to embrace your Facebook Live mistakes and keep choosing your discussion no matter what has happened.

When you make a mistake it highlights the reality that you are human much like your viewers. No one is going to dislike you for making mistakes. Mistakes can include character to your event so accept them and keep going.

Get aid with Questions

If you are anticipating high viewing numbers with your event then you need to line up some aid with the questions you will receive. It can be extremely difficult trying to make your discussion and needing to check out and answer questions as you are doing this.

So we advise that you have another person checked out the comments and reply to them. This person needs to know what they are discussing so that they can address any questions properly.

When your audience asks a question, be sure to call them out by their first name. This will help you to create an even stronger connection with your audience. Individuals that ask the questions will feel excellent that you called them out and it will encourage others to ask questions too.

Have a Call to Action at the end

You must ask your Facebook Live audiences to do something at the end of your event. So think of what you want your audiences to do once your event is over. Do you desire them to join your email list or have a look at an offer that you have at the minute?

Whatever you desire them to do make sure and tell them. If you don't tell them what to do then the probability is that they will do nothing. You can include a link under your video so tell them to click this and take the needed action. Constantly thank your audiences for enjoying your live event at the end.

Add a Custom Thumbnail

When you add a compelling thumbnail to your Facebook Live event you ought to encourage more people to go to. As soon as your event goes live your thumbnail is the most popular thing that people will see.

After your live event, your taped video will appear on your Facebook page. You can then modify this post and this is the time to include your engaging thumbnail. Facebook will pick an image from your event if you don't do this which will most likely not be as engaging as you would want it to be.

Add Captions to your Event Video

If you add captions to your event video then you should bring in a lot more audiences. Often people will see your video in their newsfeed but it will not be convenient for them to enjoy as it is late in the evening or they are outdoors in a loud environment.

A lot of people tend to see Facebook videos without sound these days so providing captions is a must. You can create your SRT declare your captions or you can have Facebook create them immediately. Constantly examine that your captions match what is being said in your event video.

Pin your Video Post

By pinning your event video post you can make it appear at the top of your Facebook page. This is a great way to get more eyeballs on your video and people to see the recording. Visitors to your page are constantly visiting what is on top so make the most of this.

Consider Boosting your Event Video

If you are happy with how things ended up with your Facebook Live event you can spend for a post-boost once the recording is on your Facebook page. You will have the ability to specify your audience utilizing several different factors such as age variety, gender, area, interests, and more.

Get an embed link for your tape-recorded event video and utilize this on your website or blog site and other social media accounts to drive more traffic to it. Never think that after you have taped your live event that your work is done. It has only just started.

Usage Facebook Analytics

A few days after your event you need to take a look at the insights on Facebook for your event video to see how well it did or didn't do. You will see all of the normal video metrics such as several unique views, comments, shares, average time was seen, and so on.

As this was a Facebook Live video there will be extra metrics as well such as the peak number of views, average view time, the reach of the video, and demographic information. Use all of this information to make improvements in your next Facebook Live event.

In the next chapter, we will discuss the brand-new Facebook Live includes for 2021 …

CHAPTER 5

FACEBOOK LIVE NEW FEATURES FOR 2021

Facebook is always searching for ways to improve its features to help businesses and in 2020 there were several new functions added to Facebook Live. Here are the exciting features that they have included:

The Trimming Feature

With the trimming feature, you will have the ability to modify the start and the end of your live event tape-recorded video. Regularly, the start of live events has empty areas that you don't wish to appear in the recorded video. Users of Facebook Live requested that they could include a "standby page" and this has now appeared.

The start of your event video is crucial. If nothing is going on then some audiences are most likely to leave. It will irritate those that remain and they might begin to dislike your event. So use the brand-new trim feature so that you can make the start of your event videos better and remove any useless video at the end.

Duration now Extended

This is a brand-new feature that may not be of any effect to you at all however we wished to make you familiar with it. The maximum duration time for a Facebook Live event has been extended from 4 hours to eight hours.

Facebook made this change in action to some broadcasters that required it such as those that utilize Facebook Live for sporting events, news events, and so on.

It is very not likely that you will want to create an event anywhere near 8 hours long for your business and brand. We strongly advise that you do not make your events too long.

Watch Parties

This is a new feature that you need to bear in mind. People usually like to see a video together with friends and family and now you can utilize this feature for your Facebook Live events. Studies by Facebook have revealed that when people view a video with family and friends they are likely to leave a comment by as much as 8 times more than they would if they were watching a Facebook video alone.

You can now arrange a watch party from your Facebook page before your Facebook Live event starting. An announcement post is generated when you use this feature and your audience can opt-in to receive an alert about when your celebration (your event) begins. Facebook has likewise added some useful brand-new metrics for watch celebrations.

You can now see the minutes viewed and there is likewise a distinct 60s see metric. This exposes the variety of special audiences that have watched a minimum of 60 seconds of the watch celebration. So benefit from the brand-new watch celebration function for your Facebook Live events.

In the next chapter, we will go over content concepts for your Facebook Live events ...

CHAPTER 6

GREAT CONTENT IDEAS FOR YOUR FACEBOOK LIVE EVENTS

Now that you understand Facebook Live can be a terrific tool for promoting your business and your brand how will you use it? Coming up with new content ideas for Facebook Live isn't always simple so in this chapter, we have some great ideas for you so that you can develop some amazing live events and market your business.

The How-To Event

There are always numerous searches online for "how-to" type videos. People like to watch a video to find out how to do something and you can give your audience what it desires by developing Facebook Live events around recognized problems and supply the responses that they need.

When you produce a live event video that helps your audience they will certainly appreciate it. Not just are you likely to receive a lot of positive comments and likes, however, a great deal of the audiences will share your event video with their followers.

People will frequently watch a good how-to video more than once. They might not have got all of the info that they required from the very first watching and require to return and see it again. So think of the how-to videos that you can produce using Facebook Live to keep your audience happy and make them share with others.

New Product Launches

A lot of businesses effectively use Facebook Live to announce the launch of a new service or product.

You can get the news out about your new launch extremely quickly with live video. Develop a live event to let your audience know that your new product or service is coming soon. Make sure to develop anticipation and excitement throughout the event.

As quickly as your service or product is ready produce a Facebook Live event around it. Welcome, all of the people that attended your very first event so that you will optimize your chances of making sales. Make certain that you respond to any questions that viewers have in both events.

Professional Interviews

If there are specialists in your niche that will be willing to participate in an interview with you then you can make this a Facebook Live event. This type of event is usually useful to you along with the professional.

Ask the professional to notify all of his fans (including their email list and on other social accounts) when the vent is occurring and what will be gone over. Your specialist will know people that you don't and vice versa. When you are just beginning you will benefit more, but over time this will even itself out.

Services Or Product Demonstrations

This will work well for a lot of specific niches. Let's state that you offer a software product, you can use Facebook Live to show the various functions of your product. Possibly you have added brand-new functions and want to get the word out about these quick. Facebook Live is the perfect method to do this.

Demonstrating the functions of a service or product is going to assist you to offer more of it. People do not constantly take notice of product functions and when you enlighten them with a Facebook Live event you have a higher chance of transforming them.

Ask Me Anything or Q&A

This is an excellent idea for Facebook Live content once you have established your brand. People like these types of live events and they will generally have high levels of interaction. A live questions and answers session always decreases well.

You can structure these events around particular issues that your audience has. For example, they might want to know how they can generate more traffic to their website. To create a live event that will answer questions from your audience around this. By thoroughly picking your subjects you can keep your audience focused and get higher levels of engagement.

In the next chapter, we will discuss how you can produce the most interesting Facebook Live events ...

CHAPTER 7

CREATING THE MOST ENGAGING FACEBOOK LIVE EVENTS

To develop truly appealing Facebook Live events there are things that you require to do before the event, during the event, and after the event. You will supply your brand with a well-deserved increase if you produce interesting events and all it needs is some idea and a following a few basic actions.

Unfortunately, there are numerous examples of bad Facebook Live videos around. These videos look like they were an afterthought or a business simply going through the motions. They are boring and uninspiring. We do not want you to produce these types of events so follow the steps below and produce appealing events rather.

Develop your Event around what your Audience desires

The more that you know your audience the better. They will voluntarily inform you what they desire in regards to content for your next Facebook Live event if you ask. When you can develop a Facebook Live event that assists people to resolve the problems that they have then your audience will like it.

Engaging Facebook Live events are interesting for the audience. If you wish to delight your audience then ask to select the subject of your next event. You can ask straight, run surveys and polls and develop the style of your event around typical questions that your audience has about the specific niche.

Arrange your Event and Promote it first

You wish to develop as much anticipation for your Facebook Live event as you can. So we suggest that you arrange your event for the following week and after that use the time before to promote as hard as possible.

If you develop a helpful video for YouTube or write a terrific article then you will publish it first and after that promote. However, it doesn't work that way with Facebook Live. You want to get as many people to see the live event as you can so promotion before it occurs is the very best technique.

You can create posts on Facebook about your approaching event and after that improve these posts so that you extend your reach to people that are not your fans yet. This is inexpensive to do and can be highly efficient. Target your audience specifically and make your post appealing and you will get excellent outcomes.

We advise that with each post you make about your upcoming event you share something various about it with your audience. Don't just utilize the same message over and over again. Speak about some important details that you will share and consist of various pointers in each post.

Do not simply use Facebook to tell the world about your next Facebook Live event. If you have other social channels then utilize these to get people excited about it. Send out emails out to your email list telling them about your event. Publish posts on your blog site about it. Utilize every channel that you have available.

Prepare your Environment

The primary difference between Facebook Live events and live streaming on YouTube is that Facebook is viewed as more "easy-going". A YouTube live event tends to be a lot more serious. Despite this, you want to remove as many distractions as you can to produce the most engaging Facebook Live events.

We suggest that you forget about the "easy-going" track record that Facebook Live events have and try to develop the most expert production that you can. After all, this is your business and your brand and you do not want it to be a shambles. More people are going to watch a live event than they are a basic video so put your best foot forward.

Examine your environment before you begin recording. Are there things in your environment that could sidetrack your viewers? How great is the lighting? What does the audio sound like? You can do a test tape-recording to look for all of these things and then make any subsequent modifications.

Broadcasting against a plain background can work well. If you have a background that has a great deal of mess in it then your audience can be very distracted by this. So keep it very little. You want your audiences to concentrate on you and what you need to say.

Timing is everything

If you perform your Facebook Live broadcast at the incorrect time then you will seriously minimize the number of viewers. You need to do your research on where your audience is located and figure out the very best time for your event.

If you arrange your Facebook Live event for a time where most of your audience is working then you will get miserable viewing figures. The figures will be even worse if you hold your event when your audience is normally sleeping.

Facebook Live is an international tool that you can use to boost your brand name no matter where you lie worldwide. If you live in Europe and your target market is North America then you might need to make sacrifices.

You might need to run events that are late in the day for you however are timed well for your audience. Remember it is about them and not you.

Keep Updating your Audience

Now we enjoy pointers for engaging Facebook Live videos throughout the event. One thing that you always need to remember is that people can join your event at any time. Not everybody is going to exist from the start, so you require to make statements at different times during your event so that everybody depends on the date.

So you can say things like "welcome if you have just recently joined us. We are discussing XYZ at the moment and before that, we talked about ABC". You get the idea. It's constantly a great idea to share a program for your event with your audiences so they know what to anticipate. This will help to keep them seeing your event for the longest possible time.

Interaction is King

We have discussed the reality that you need a good level of interaction in your Facebook Live events a couple of times in this guide and the reason for this is that it is so essential for a genuinely appealing event. A lot of people that participate in Facebook Live events wish to connect with the host so don't deprive them of this.

You wish to give your audience the feeling that your event is truly a two-way discussion with you and your business. People leave comments on a Facebook Live event more than ten times more than typical videos.

Make certain that all of the comments show up live with your event. When others see these comments they will be more likely to share their thoughts. You will probably require some help here.

Comments can be available in thick and quick and if you have somebody assisting you they can make you familiar with the most common styles etc

React to comments as quickly as you can. An option to this is to have a session at the end where you will resolve them. This is the same as a question and answers session which can be very efficient. People need to know that you take their viewpoints seriously and responding to their comments is the best way to do this.

Give some shoutouts with your event. When your event ends up the recording will be offered and you can bring attention to this by sharing a post thanking all those that attended your event for example. Attempt asking people for a lot more comments and questions about your event. They will feel good about this and it will help to increase engagement.

Utilize your Events to Build Relationships

Do not utilize your Facebook Live events as one long series of advertisements. There are different manner ins which you can promote your product or services utilizing Facebook Live and we will cover these in the next chapter. Concentrate on establishing a strong relationship with your audience.

Some of the audiences to your live events will not have heard of you or your brand prior. So you require to seize the day of structure trust with them. You require to treat each event like you are attempting to make an excellent first impression.

Promote your Video after the event

Take every chance that you can to promote your taped event video to those that did not participate in life. Make a post on your site about it and use other channels to get the word out. If you have a YouTube channel then you can publish the video there too.
Don't overdo it with this. The majority of people have a Facebook account however not everybody has and you might discover this holds with some

of your list customers for example. That is why adding your video to YouTube where anyone can view it is essential.

What can you do better?

When your event is over go through your recording to see how well you carried it out.
Did you come across it in a friendly way?
What mistakes did you make?
Did anything fail?
You can always do things much better the next time around.

Use the metrics available on Facebook to see how many people attended the event and what your reach was. Facebook has a lot of insightful metrics that we motivate you to use after your events. Discover all of them and utilize them regularly.

In the next chapter, we will discuss how you can utilize Facebook Live to drive leads and sales ...

CHAPTER 8

HOW TO USE FACEBOOK LIVE TO DRIVE LEADS AND SALES

You can utilize Facebook Live to drive leads for your business and create sales. While this is possible, you need to use the ideal approach for success. So we have some fantastic suggestions for you here so that you can maximize the number of leads that you produce from your Facebook Live events and the variety of sales too.

Usage Promotions and Discounts during your Events

This may appear apparent to you, but it is amazing the number of businesses that host Facebook Live events forget to speak about their promotions and discount rate offers. Live videos are a great way to create leads and make sales so you should include these things in your events.

You do not want to go crazy with this. Just mention your promos and discount rate deals once in a while. Maybe you have a free offer that will benefit your audience. Warm your viewers up about this at the start of your event and after that share the details halfway through and once again at the end.

Discount rate offers are effective and a lot of people that attend a Facebook Live event from a business will be expecting this. So don't dissatisfy them and be clear about what the discount is and how audiences can obtain it.

Use Prompts for Lead Generation

You need a good sales to funnel set up to support your Facebook Live event. Then you require to steer your audiences into your funnel. You want to record their e-mail address so that they join your list so provide the download of something valuable free of charge for instance.

Inform your event audiences what you are going to cover in your video. The most effective Facebook Live events share value at the start and after that pitch a related deal. You want your audience to stay for the pitch so make this as interesting as possible for them. Tell them that it will solve a particular problem and it deserves hanging on for.

Using prompts as you lead up to your pitch is usually extremely efficient. You want your audiences to connect with you so ask a question like "if you are excited then let us understand in the comments" or "if you would like to know more about our items then please type "yes please" in the comments".

After the event, you can follow up straight with those that reacted to your triggers. You understand that they are interested so the follow-up will be quite simple. Be sure to follow up as soon after the event as possible when the leads are the hottest.

Show your Products or Services

Absolutely nothing offers a service or product much better than a live demonstration. So take the opportunity that Facebook Live offers you to do this. When your audience sees what your service or product can do for them they will be a lot most likely to need to know more or make a purchase right now.

Plan your demonstration. What features of the services or product do you wish to highlight? What will have the greatest effect on the audience? How will your services or product conserve time and/or money? Only demonstrate one of your services or products live at each event.

Don't try to demonstrate your whole range! We recommend that you offer value in your event first by discussing how your audience can overcome a particular problem that they have. Then show your product and services showing them how they can resolve their issue a lot more quickly and save time and possibly money.

So for instance, if you offer products or services that help people produce traffic to their website you can show them some manual ways to drive traffic first and explain how time-consuming these methods are. Then you can introduce and demonstrate your service or product which automates the methods and saves time.

Strong Call to Action

You require to inform your event viewers what you want them to do. The best way to attain this is with strong calls to action during your event and later. Never assume that somebody watching your event will understand instinctively what you desire them to do. Spell it out with a persuasive call to action.

Include your call to action in the event recording post too. Make a comment that advises people about it. It will not take a great deal of time to set this up and it is worth it because you are most likely to generate more leads.

Ask your Viewers to Share your Event

If your audience is enjoying your live event then they will more than happy to share it with people that they know. A few of them will simply do this naturally, but it is constantly best to ask them to share your event throughout your discussion.

This can extend the reach of your Facebook Live marketing project. Make your audience part of your marketing group. You might provide a reward for sharing your events such as a discount rate or free download for example.

In the next chapter, we will share the very best practices that you need to follow to get the most out of Facebook Live for your business ...

CHAPTER 9

FACEBOOK LIVE BEST PRACTICES

Here are the 8 finest practices that we highly recommend that you follow to produce the best Facebook Live events to promote your business. You can improve your brand and drive a lot of leads and sales from Facebook Live events. We believe that if you follow these finest practices you will have the optimum possibility of success.

Understand what Facebook Live is

You must understand what the Facebook Live platform is and how you can use it to provide your brand an increase and boost leads and sales for your business. Facebook users are far more most likely to view a live event than they are a prerecorded video or a basic post including text and images. You can use Facebook Live on a computer system or mobile device.

Advantages of Facebook Live

You need to be familiar with the benefits of using Facebook Live in your marketing strategy. Facebook is the biggest social network platform by a long way and has billions of users. When you utilize Facebook Live properly you can develop a great connection with your audience. There is some terrific analytics also.

Get going the right way with Facebook Live

You must take your Facebook Live events seriously. This starts by making a financial investment in the ideal webcam and microphone to produce high-quality events. Make sure that your WiFi signal is strong before you record. You need to prepare your Facebook Live events and it is much better to schedule them beforehand so you have time to promote them.

Usage Proven methods to develop a Great Facebook Live Event

There are things that you need to do before, throughout, and after your Facebook Live event to get the very best outcomes. Before taping your live event you require to guarantee that you utilize the ideal lighting. Produce a couple of practice recordings so that you can examine whatever.

Throughout your event be as human as possible and smile often. Learn to smile when you are speaking so that you stumble upon yourself well. Be sure to ask your audience to connect with you and constantly learn from any mistakes. Always utilize strong calls to action in your events.

After your event, you require to promote your recording. Include captions to it so that more people will see it. Consider increasing your recording post to extend your reach. Produce a customized thumbnail for your recording that attracts users to see it.

Maintain to date with New Features

Facebook is constantly upgrading their Facebook Live platform to make it better for its users. They are constantly adding brand-new features and you must be aware of these. In 2020 they included a helpful cutting function, extended the recording duration, and introduced the Watch Party function.

Usage Good Content Ideas

If your Facebook Live event consists of good content then you will get more audiences and higher levels of engagement. You can develop "how-to" events, product launches, interview specialists, show your services and products, and run question and answer sessions.

Produce Engaging Facebook Live Events

Engaging Facebook Live events are the most effective. Find out what your audience wants and develop events around this. Make sure that your environment is right for your event and schedule it at the best times.

Update your audience frequently during your event and encourage them to engage with you. Evaluate your events, later on, to see what you can do better.

Drive Leads and Sales with Facebook Live

Use techniques to drive more leads and sales during your Facebook Live events. Inform your audience about any promotions and discount deals. Set up a sales funnel and after that use prompts throughout your event to drive viewers to it. Always include a strong call to action in your events. Ask your audience to share your event.

CONCLUSION

If you have read this guide from start to finish you will have a mutual understanding of how you can use Facebook Live for the benefit of your business. You mustn't simply jump onto the platform without understanding what you are doing.

Now it is over to you. While reading this guide will make you a bit smarter, just by taking action will you have the ability to utilize the Facebook Live platform to enhance your brand and drive more leads and sales.

We hope that you found this guide to be informative and helpful. Get going today with your Facebook Live marketing. We wish you every success promoting your business on the world's biggest social platform!

www.ingramcontent.com/pod-product-compliance
Lightning Source LLC
Chambersburg PA
CBHW031552210526
45464CB00003B/1274